STILL STANDING

STILL STANDING

Contents

Dedication vii

1
Table of Contents 1

2
Acknowledgements 2

3
Foreword 4

4
Introduction 10

5
The Baby Is Coming 14

6
Nap When The Baby Naps 21

7
Aww... So Cute 29

8
Sit Down and Be Still 35

9
Hide and Seek   43

10
No More Training Wheels   48

11
I Can Do All Things   54

12
When Mommy?...Soon   60

About The Author   66

This book is dedicated to all the moms faced with adversities, yet giving motherhood their all and "still standing".

This book is dedicated to every person "still standing" on God's promises despite what they see with their physical eyes.

This book is dedicated to everyone who may not yet be where they want to be, but are "still standing".

Copyright © 2021 by Shuranda Hall

All rights reserved. No part of this book may be reproduced in any manner whatsoever without written permission except in the case of brief quotations embodied in critical articles and reviews.

"Scripture quotations taken from the Amplified® Bible (AMP),
Copyright © 2015 by The Lockman Foundation
Used by permission. www.Lockman.org"

Scripture quotations marked (NLT) are taken from the Holy Bible, New Living Translation, copyright © 1996, 2004, 2007 by Tyndale House Foundation. Used by permission of Tyndale House Publishers, Inc., Carol Stream, IL 60188. All rights reserved.

Scripture taken from the New King James Version®. Copyright © 1982 by Thomas Nelson, Inc. Used by permission. All rights reserved.

ISBN 978-1-7777310-1-4
First Printing, 2021

I

Table of Contents

Acknowledgments

Introduction

The Baby Is Coming

Nap When the Baby naps

Awww… So Cute

Sit Down and Be Still

Hide and Seek

No More Training Wheels

I Can Do All Things

When Mommy? Soon…

2

Acknowledgements

To My Heavenly Father - Thank you for entrusting me with such a task as this. Many days the challenges seem very hard; but knowing that my long suffering can impact another person's life positively is very rewarding. May your will be done.

To my mother, Iris Strachan - Thank you for being an excellent example of a mother to follow. I'm very appreciative of the bond that has grown between us. Thank you for the time taken out of your busy schedule to read and reread the drafts of this book.

To my spiritual mother, Pastor Ibukun Adewusi - Thank you for sacrificing time to not only read, but to write the foreword for this book. You have taken me in as your own and I am forever grateful. May God's blessing over you life never cease.

To my husband and best friend, Alexander "Wellie" Hall - Thank you for always being an encouragement when I felt like I could not go on. Thank you for holding faith when mine was shaky. Thank you for allowing me to share a portion of our lives with the world. Having a very supportive husband has been a great blessing when I needed to separate from family affairs in order to complete this book. I love you beyond explanation.

3

Foreword

James 1:17 tells us that every good and perfect gift comes from God. In Psalms 127:3, we are reminded that children are a heritage and gift from the Lord. Since the truth is established in the mouth of two or three witnesses, we can conclude that children are a good and perfect gift and inheritance from God.

Parenting is an entrustment from God, where He is trusting a father and/or mother in raising a godly seed for His purpose. Whether you're a biological parent, spiritual parent, adopted parent, foster parent, acquired parent (In-laws) or grandparent, this is a huge entrustment from God. In 2 Timothy 1:12, it states God's expectation from us as parents.

"And this is why I am suffering as I do. Still I am not ashamed, for **I know** (perceive, have knowledge of, and am acquainted with) **Him** Whom **I have believed** (adhered to and trusted in and relied on), and **I am** [positively] **persuaded** that

He is able to guard *and* keep that **which has been entrusted to me** *and* which **I have committed [to Him] until that day.**" (2 Timothy 1:12, Amplified Classic Edition)

From this passage, we can see that we are entrusted first by God, but it is wisdom to commit what He has entrusted to us back to God and in this case, these are our children. This is the essence of child dedication, where a parent dedicates the children, He has given to them back to Him. However, in order to effectively dedicate or commit them back into His hands, there are some important steps that need to have been established, which includes knowing him, believing him and trusting in His ability to guard and keep our children.

Let's examine some responsibilities on us as parents:

Responsibilities of Parents

To Know Him

It is one thing to know about God, but it is another thing to have a personal relationship with God. This is knowing Him for yourself. What nature of God have you personally experienced in your life as a parent or as a believer? Let's take for example the faithfulness of God. God is a faithful God even when we are not faithful. If He has said it, He is faithful to do fulfil it. What experiences have you experienced in your life where God truly showed His faithfulness to you. E.g., securing a job, a home, having children, preserving your life from an accident. As you ponder on the faithfulness of God in those personal experiences of yours, it solidifies your confidence in God, which brings us to believing in Him.

To Believe Him

Believing in God is not just a one-time thing. It is a lifestyle of faith that needs to be cultivated. The bible says in Romans 10:17 that faith comes by hearing, and hearing by the word of God. Our faith and belief in God grow as we hear the word of God, which can be in different forms including, the written word of God, anointed messages/sermons, words of testimonies. As we ponder on the words that we hear from God, our faith rises, and it strengthens our faith in God. Testimonies are very powerful because they are resumes of God's work in our lives and in the lives of others and helps fortify our faith in God.

To Trust in His Ability to Guard and Keep

Before we go to a restaurant or a hotel or on a vacation resort, we tend to look at the past track records of those places, which we call reviews. We look at the reviewing ratings and comments from past visitors to those places, which can determine if we will be visiting those spots. Likewise, it is wisdom to look at the past records of God in guarding and keeping things or people. For example, when we look at the story of Jesus, we can see that though a target was placed on His head right from young, the Lord was always one step ahead of the enemy in preserving the life of Jesus, from the hand of Herod who wanted to kill Jesus, by directing the wise men to take a different route and not return to Herod. Moses is another example of a child kept by God. When Pharaoh ordered for every male Hebrew boy to be killed at birth, the Lord preserved the life of Moses, ensuring that the midwives given the order did not obey such order and allowed the boys to live. Even when it seemed like Moses' mother could no longer hide him, God made sure that Pharaoh's daughter saw Moses where he was placed in the basket and decided to take care of him as her own.

To Commit our Children Back to God

Isaiah 52:12 reminds us that God will go before us and will be our rear guard. I love this verse because it is a reminder that we do not need to do the watching of our back or the backs of our children. God has decided to take that responsibility, but it is our responsibility to hand them over to God. Just like in a wrestling match, where the only way a wrestler can take advantage of the extra support of the wrestler outside of the ring by shaking them, the same goes with parenting. If we do not involve God and commit our children back to God, God will not force His way into our lives or our children's lives. We must give Him permission by allowing Him to take charge over their lives. Remember, these children are primarily God's children and we as parents are only stewards over them. It is wisdom to allow God to direct the affairs of their lives and align ourselves to His perfect plan and will for their lives. He is the one who wrote the scripts of their lives, and He is willing and able to care for them.

Responsibilities of God

To Entrust us with Our Children

Having children is a gift from God and not by the doing of any man. This does not mean we cannot take advantage of assisted reproductive treatments such as Intrauterine Insemination (IUI) or In Vitro Fertilization (IVF) and the likes, but the ultimate one that decides if a child would be an outcome, is God. As we look at past track records of the faithfulness of God in bringing about conception of children, against all odds, I am assured that if He did it before, He will do it again. He did it in the life of Sarah, that had gone way past menopause and God caused her to laugh by giving her son at the age of 90. Hannah is another lady that God remembered her prayer and gave her Samuel. Rachel's womb was opened by God, and He gave her Joseph and lest we forget Elizabeth, who gave birth to John, the Baptist. Regardless of how long it seems it has been, it is not over until God says it is over. When you look at these children born, despite the delays, they were phenomenal children of great destinies. Just like it sometimes takes a bit longer in preparing a special meal order, so it is sometimes, when God is carving out special delivery children. So, when the thoughts come about whether you will conceive or not, tell the devil, God is taking His time in preparing my phenomenal children. Hold on to God's promise in Exodus 23:26 "None shall lose her young by miscarriage or be barren in your land; I will fulfill the number of your days." (Amplified).

To Guard and Keep Them Once Committed Back to Him

As we trust God in committing our children back to Him, He is faithful to guard and keep our children from harm. He that never sleeps nor slumber, will constantly keep His eyes over our children and watch them. That is God's promise to us.

"And this is why I am suffering as I do. Still I am not ashamed, for **I know** (perceive, have knowledge of, and am acquainted with) **Him** Whom **I have believed** (adhered to and trusted in and relied on), and **I am** [positively] **persuaded** that **He is able to guard** *and* **keep** that **which has been entrusted to me** *and* which **I have committed [to Him] until that day.**" (2 Timothy 1:12, Amplified Classic Edition)

As you take the time to read this book, you will find practical and transparent truths that will help you in believing and trusting in the one that has entrusted you with such priceless gifts as your children. It will also show you powerful and intentional steps you can take in committing them back to God. It is my prayer that God will find us as worthy and faith stewards over His entrusted gift.

Pastor Ibukun Adewusi
Cornerstone Christian Church of God

4

Introduction

August 15, 2011

This is when Jayden was born. The doctor's words to me were, "I don't know what's going on in there, but the baby isn't growing, and we have to take him out today. He is going to spend about a month here with us." Frankly speaking, I didn't really grasp exactly what he was saying. I don't think that I understood the part about Jayden having to stay in the hospital. I somehow thought despite his early delivery, Jayden would still be coming home with me. I knew that it had been a bit of a rough road with the pregnancy.

Even though I felt fine, every time I went for a checkup, there would be concerns about Jayden's growth. This time the doctor didn't want to take any chances. He explained that it was best to deliver him as sometimes babies experiencing difficulties in the womb tend to thrive better after being born. That night I met my 3 pounds 4 ounces baby boy. Alex and

I became quite familiar with the hospital. Jayden was discharged after 28 days at 4 pounds 5 ounces.

Dec 22, 2012

"She's beautiful! But she's a little small and needs a bit of help with breathing so we will be taking her up to the NICU for a couple days." This pregnancy was pretty good, I had no issues and was expecting all to go well. Not so! After Sadé was born, she required some assistance breathing. She was given oxygen for some time and spent about 5 days in the hospital; there were no major issues. This one was hard! I had to leave Sadé in the hospital on Christmas day when I was discharged. I was a bit devastated as I felt like I was leaving my Christmas present in the hospital. Nonetheless I was grateful as 2 days after I was discharged, we were able to pick up our 5 pounder and bring her home.

August 15, 2016

"I'm so sorry, the baby has no heartbeat. You are having a miscarriage". This was my third pregnancy, and I should have been about 12 weeks along. But there was no heartbeat. I left the hospital and went home to continue preparing for Jayden's birthday party; it was his birthday that day. I had to pass the fetus naturally and I was in excruciating pain. I was in even more pain emotionally. But I had to show up for Jayden.

May 13, 2017

"Ma'am, I don't know what's happening, but your baby's heartbeat is quite low, and we need to perform an emergency C-Section." This one is Haylie's story. Alex and I had gone to dinner. This was supposed to be the last big date before the baby came. We were out to dinner and things quickly shifted. This feeling was different. Unknowingly, I was undergoing a placental abruption. The placenta was literally pulling itself away from my uterus, and the pain was unbearable.

Haylie was born that night. She was just over 5 pounds. She wasn't breathing when she was born and had to be resuscitated. It took 8 minutes to bring her back; resuscitation at birth usually ends at 10 minutes. After that, the child is considered still born. She had 2 minutes left. The lack of oxygen caused a serious brain injury for Haylie. I lost a lot of blood and had to be given blood transfusions – 3 bags total. I spent 5 days in the hospital; Haylie spent one month in the hospital and has been fighting against the odds ever since. Nonetheless, I am confident that this battle is already won.

Nov 2, 2018

I was probably the most nervous I'd ever been. I wanted to be at peace; I knew I needed to be, but it was hard to do so. I kept thinking of my past 3 childbirth stories. God taught me this day, that the past does not dictate the future. Josiah was born healthy, just over 6 pounds. We were both discharged on November 4th, 2018. I had never taken any of my babies home the same day that I left the hospital.

This was a first and I was grateful.

5

The Baby Is Coming

This chapter is about preparation… you've geared and prepared for this child but then the unexpected happened…but if you were prepared, would it be unexpected? What is preparation for motherhood all about?

There is an unexpected part of motherhood extending beyond the lullabies, the cute baby clothes, and new baby scent. These are times when you would wonder, and ask God "what did I ever do wrong? Why are you putting me through this?" Yet, these are the times that push you to trust God more than ever before – the unexpected challenges that make you strong and push your faith to unlimited measures.

For many mothers, these challenges can look different; but the same God that has been keeping me will keep you.

To be honest, I don't feel like I am capable of even talking about motherhood. There are some days when I don't feel like

I was a good mother. There are many days when I feel like I failed the kids, or my task at hand. But I understand that emotions are temporary and what God thinks of me matters more than my feelings. I must trust the fact that God is in control, and that He blessed me with these children. He lent them to me, for me to take care of them. So even though many times I don't trust myself, I don't feel capable myself, I believe, and stand on the truth that God believes I'm capable.

As expectant mothers, we are encouraged to get ready for baby: get the crib, stroller, car seat; pick out registry items for a shower; prepare baby's room; take maternity photos or get a belly cast...and the list goes on and on. For me and my husband Alex, it was "let's go out to dinner, it will probably be the last time we get to be out without a diaper bag for a while!" We had two other kids at this time, but they were 4 and 5 years old and out of diaper stage and able to carry their own snack bags when we went out. But here we were again... we had been surprised with a baby shower, had all the room and crib prepared, and my mom had even taken off the time from work in order to come and help me and baby. We were oh so prepared for anything! And what we weren't prepared for, we figured we would just wing it, after all we weren't new parents...we had done this twice before...we had this in the bag. Or so we thought!

It was that same night we were going for dinner, our last date night for a bit, when things shifted. Hubby had picked a fancy restaurant that was quite pricy, and not our go to place with 2 kids, but this was a special occasion, right? My friend's daughter came over to baby sit and I got as dolled up as I could with my pregnancy discolored skin and swollen nose, and we went out to chow down. I don't know if we had even received our first course yet before things began to change. Though I had 2 children already, they had both been cesarean sections and I hadn't the privilege of experiencing labor before. I told my husband that something felt different, and I think I was in labor but that I wasn't sure. In a matter of minutes, that feeling went from I think this is labor to agonizing pain... something is happening. That "last important dinner" was cut short, and Alex and I headed to the hospital.

I remember when I entered the hospital room, one of the nurses saying, "wow you look really nice to be coming to the hospital". I had always joked with my husband that this pregnancy I was going to apply makeup before I went in to deliver so I would be picture ready. (Well, that's a perfect example of the power of the tongue). The nurse immediately hooked me up to a machine to monitor baby and tried to discretely call for the doctor on duty. I sensed something was up...I wasn't sure what, but I knew this was not normal. I immediately whispered to Alex "pray, something is up, and this baby is coming tonight."

Many pokes and prodding later I was being wheeled into the operating room for an emergency "C-section". I remember the doctor's words clearly "Ma'am I don't know what's happening but, your baby's heartbeat is extremely low, and we have to take her out now!" I was still calm; I mean I had two previous C-sections before, and these doctors are professionals, right? Well, little did I know I had had a placental abruption causing baby girl to suffer a brain injury due to the lack of oxygen for an extended amount of time. It was when Alex came and said to me that the doctors were transferring my baby to another hospital with a better equipped NICU that the emotions hit.

My previous two births had resulted in NICU stays. The first for a month, and the second for a week. I was so excited this time to finally have baby in the room with me! To spend time bonding with my human baby and not an electric breast pump on a 3-hour schedule. All my dreams came crashing down when I heard the news of the transfer. I still did not really know at this time what happened to baby, but I remember crying because not only were we not going to be in the same room, but not even the same hospital this time! Alex then whispered to me "this isn't our fight, this is God's". To be honest that comment didn't immediately settle me. My thoughts were more along the line of, "Seriously? Again?"

Due to the abruption and the surgery, I had lost lots of blood and required blood transfusions. I continued to hemorrhage internally and ended up being transferred to the same hospital Haylie had been transferred to for critical care. This is when I was allowed to see baby. She was hooked up to everything! I had spent lots of time in the NICU prior; but this? This was different! I couldn't hold my baby girl. Her major organs had experienced some form of organ failure; the doctors had begun performing treatments to preserve the organs. I couldn't imagine such a tiny specimen needing all those different medications. This is when the NICU head doctor said that he doesn't know if she will make it through the night.

Can I tell you at this point is when all the physical preparation that were made previously goes out of the window? This juncture is where you really need to be prepared. This is by no means meant to frighten any mother-to-be, but to emphasize that being prepared goes way beyond the physical collection and organization of "cute clothes" and "fancy strollers". You are about to bring a human being into this world – one who is destined for greatness and the enemy doesn't like that! Can I tell you that, he hates you mother for the role you play in birthing "a child whom God has created for greatness"? You must be so prepared for the unexpected that it is expected! Let me elaborate. You are not being anxious that something bad will happen, and I pray you will never experience anything like this in Jesus' name! Rather you MUST understand that the enemy will always be after your children. It's his job. And it is our job to ensure that he will never be able to succeed in Jesus Name!

This type of preparedness I'm speaking about is spiritual. The good thing about this part is it is never too early to start! You may not be ready yet for kids, you may be trying to conceive, you may be pregnant, or you may have a child who is thirteen years old – in all situations this aspect is relevant! If we desire the role of motherhood, our spiritual preparedness must be given priority above the physical or materialistic preparations that we have practiced for so long.

As parents no matter what stage we are in - being spiritually proactive is more important than having diapers available for a whole year. This is a learning process and by no means am I suggesting that I have arrived or have mastered parenting or motherhood. I confess that there were times I messed up by saying the wrong things or by neglecting to make kingdom/biblical declarations over my children; when I should have, I did not make the time to pray for and with our children. When you neglect the spiritual duties over your family it allows the enemy to slip in - it's harder to fight back. Proactivity is always better than being reactive.

Was I prepared for this? Was my family – husband and children - prepared for this? Well, no one can really be prepared for such a traumatic event, right? No. But was I spiritually prepared and ready for the unexpected? I wasn't. I was caught up. Caught up imagining what it would be like to finally hold my baby right after she was born. Caught up wondering if I should wear makeup for the delivery or not. Yes, I anointed my tummy every day - well most days. Yes, I declared blessings over my baby (especially since I had just suffered a miscarriage the previous year). But I was still caught up. Don't get me wrong- it's your moment; love in it; enjoy it. But understand your priorities while preparing. Covering your child daily in prayer, declaring that every single plan of God for their life will be fulfilled; and that the enemy's plan can never prevail is more important than building a crib or painting a room blue. Being prepared, means you are spiritually ready for whatever comes.

My question to you is how prepared are you for the unexpected? What spiritual preparations are you engaging in? What changes do you need to make to prepare for the birth of your newborn?

6

Nap When The Baby Naps

This chapter is about rest – physically and emotionally. It is about resting and finding peace in God despite the challenges...

Is our rest completely over after giving birth to children? Many people would suggest that once you have children, rest as you know it is over. During pregnancy and infancy, your sleep may be interrupted due to the many changes in your body and the needs of your baby. More so, with so many hormonal changes, your peace and confidence can be affected as well. You may have worries about giving birth to a healthy child without complications; the toddler years can bring about anxiety about the possibility of your child hurting himself/herself as he/she learns to move around and discover the world. I have even heard parents, mostly mothers, complain that during the teenage years and early adulthood, their sleep is still interrupted. Why? Because they are still worrying about their children.

I'm sure that many of you may have heard the following saying before, whether you are a mom already or a mom to be: "Rest while the baby is sleeping". To be honest, this is harder than it seems. With a newborn there is always something to be done, and when babe is down for a nap and there is quiet time, it is sometimes hard to decide between taking a nap or tackling a necessary task – doing the laundry, washing the dishes, pumping breast milk, or preparing dinner. Many times, if you opt not to rest, more than likely when baby awakes from napping, you may regret – even if just a little bit – that you didn't take those few minutes or hours to rest or sleep.

Throughout this chapter however, there is a type of rest that I would like to encourage you to take. That rest is "resting in God". In Exodus 33:14, we learn about rest that comes from God.

> *"The LORD replied, "My Presence will go with you, and I will give you rest.""*

Moses was leading the Israelites to the promised land as God had instructed, but he was getting a bit frustrated as the Israelites were getting rebellious, complaining, and grumbling a whole lot! Moses still believed that God had called him to this task, and He still believed that God was with him. But Moses wanted and needed reassurance from God. He wanted to know details; how was God going to lead them? Who was God going to send with him? Moses wanted a bit more clarity on the journey ahead. God simply responded to Moses by telling him, that He will go with him, and He will give him rest. In essence, what God was saying to Moses, was that Moses should trust Him, even if he didn't know all the details; and more importantly, that he should remain at peace. God wanted Moses to know that this task, even though a heavy one, was not given to him with the intention of bringing stress or frustration. Yes, Moses was leading a group of people that had become grumblers and complainers. No, he didn't know all the details of the journey beforehand. Nonetheless, God wanted Moses to remain stress free and remember that He was with him. The New Living Translation version words it:

"I will PERSONALLY go with you, Moses".

Moses' question wasn't 'God will you go with me'? He had asked God who was He sending with him. And God's response was that He Himself was joining Moses for the journey. How exciting!? Wow! God Himself was going with Moses.

Like Moses, God has also taken it upon Himself to personally join us during this exciting journey of motherhood. How wonderful is it to know that we can have our creator and our children's creator along with us for the ride? Pardon me. It's not just "the ride", it's our life's journey. Just like Moses, during child rearing, we don't know every detail of the journey. Yes, we pray and ask God to reveal to us certain things about our children to ensure we steer them in the right direction. But He doesn't give us every single detail of their life ahead of time. Yet, He expects us to rest; to rest in Him; to trust that He will take care of us and our children.

In Psalm 121:4 we read that the Father neither slumbers nor sleeps. He is always awake, always watching. This awesome quality of our heavenly Father allows us to be able to sleep knowing that all will be well. But even more importantly, while we are awake it gives us the ability to rest; to remain at peace; to "mother" our children stress free. The things He can see and protect our children from are far greater than what we can see even when we are physically awake.

God did not intend for mothers to constantly worry about their children - worrying if they are going to meet their milestones at the recommended stage; worrying if their growth rate is in the normal range; worrying if they are being bullied at school; worrying if they are going to get caught up in the wrong crowd; worrying if they would find love. etc. God's intent is for us to be completely at peace. Allowing Him to direct the ride knowing that all is and will be well. Unfortunately, society has normalized "a mother's worry". In fact, you would probably be looked at as a bit strange if you made it known to other parents that you were not worried about "the normal worrisome parenting things".

As a mother it is indeed your responsibility to be concerned about the issues regarding your child, however it should never come to the point of worry. Worry is when you allow anxiety or uneasiness to take over; when you allow your mind to dwell on difficulty or troubles. When you do this in fact you are acting in disobedience. The bible tells us in Philippians 4:6-7 "Don't worry about anything; instead, pray about everything. Tell God what you need and thank him for all he has done. 7 Then you will experience God's peace, which exceeds anything we can understand. His peace will guard your hearts and minds as you live in Christ Jesus."

Your children are in fact first God's children. We are meant to be mere stewards over them; being entrusted with their care for a particular time. Especially if we have taken the opportunity to have them blessed by a pastor or priest, christening them into the Christian church. Even though this act has somewhat become a tradition for many, what we are really saying is "Father, thank you for blessing me with this child, but I now give him/her back to you."

Would you stress or worry about something that you have given away to someone else? If you do, you probably haven't truly given that thing away or fully given up your original rights to it. When we begin to look at our children as God's children, finding rest in Him becomes easier. We are only vessels that He has found capable and worthy of raising His children for this time. This grants us responsibility yes; but does not warrant for stress.

Let's take a moment to look at Hannah; she is a great example of "giving her child to God." Hannah had been yearning for a child for so many years. She made a vow to God that if He blessed her with a child, she would give the child back to Him. And so, God indeed blessed her with a son, and Hannah honored her word. As soon as her son had completed the stage of nursing, she took him to the temple and left him to be mentored by Eli to work for the Lord. She only visited him once a year. Talk about "giving with no strings attached"! This may seem extreme, but this was Hannah's personal vow to God. These days, as enticing as it may sound, God isn't asking us to physically drop our children off at our local church and leave them there for a whole year. Rather, He wants us to release all worries and concerns about our children into His hands and to trust Him to take care of them.

My first three children all spent time in the Neonatal Intensive Care Unit (NICU) after they were born. I can honestly say with my first-born Jayden, I did not have this understanding to cast all my worries and cares upon God. There were not any major issues going on with Jayden; he was born prematurely and because of that had to remain in the hospital for a month, until he reached a particular weight when he could be released. The medical team never seemed overly concerned about anything regarding him, as he had no health issues and was doing quite well. Oh, but I was so worried! I couldn't sleep at night knowing that my son was in the hospital, and I was at home. When he came home, I became worried that if I didn't wake him up every three hours on the hour to feed him as they did in the hospital, that he would not thrive. I was worried when they said that he was smaller than he should be at all his early doctors' checkups. What a bunch of unnecessary wasted energy and time worrying about things I had no control over. If I knew what motherhood was about to bring me, I would have used all that worry time to sleep! Hindsight!

Ironically, when Haylie was born things were much more complicated, but I was growing in Christ and had a better understanding about God's rest. Of course, there were many emotions at first and it was only by God's grace that I was able to fight off every urge to fall into a state of worry. Eventually, with the help of God and a Godly circle I found God's rest. With so many doctors and medical personnel giving their own opinion and prognosis, only the peace of God can allow one to be able to hear all the different medical views yet still stand firm on God's word that "All is well".

With so many babies unexpectedly dying from sudden infant death syndrome worldwide, only the peace of God will enable you to put your baby down to sleep knowing that all will be well. God's peace will relieve you from sitting up and worrying all night, or constantly checking every few minutes to see if your baby is breathing. The rest of God is needed when you send your children to school, not knowing who and what they will be exposed to. The rest of God is needed when you know your child is about to sit an especially important exam that will determine the direction that their future will go, and they have already expressed that they themselves are a bit nervous. God forbid a child were to get mixed up with the wrong crowd and found themselves blatantly being rebellious and perhaps even leaving home to "find themselves"; oh, here the rest of God is greatly needed.

Resting in God, in His promises, finding that peace that surpasses all understanding; whether something has already happened with your children or you are just concerned that something will or can happen is imperative in motherhood. Finding rest is a choice, it takes effort, a commitment – especially after receiving unpleasant news. Oh, but how much easier is it to focus on the parenting task at hand when you haven't allowed your mind to be overwhelmed with worry and anxiety! What a blessing to be able to parent children knowing confidently that even if something unexpected or seemingly unpleasant were to happen, our Heavenly Father is right there with you. He has all the answers and will PERSONALLY go with you and give you rest.

7

Aww... So Cute

"Oooh baby I love you! Do you love mommy? Tell mommy you love her!" These are the words that we usually coo to our little ones as soon as they are born, when they are "cute". I'm sure that there are very few moms who haven't experienced the overwhelming feelings of love and emotions when their child is little and is still "cute". So why are so many children still growing up "unloved" and seeking love in the wrong places? Yes, even the ones that came from Christian homes. We must realize that love isn't an emotion...it's a choice. And it's a choice that we must make if we intend to raise emotionally sound adults. Ok, I really must admit, this is one area that I sometimes still struggle with. A lot. I mean I tell my kids that I love them a few times a day, and before bed. That should make me an awesome mom, right? Not necessarily, just as when we are dating and we expect our special someone to show us love, our children are expecting us to SHOW them love - not just tell them. I mean, we have the perfect example, don't we?

God didn't just tell us that He loved us, He showed us love. He allowed His blameless son to die so that we can have a chance at eternal life. He would never ask us to do that! Rather, taking the time to learn your children's different love language and being intentional about expressing it is probably going to be the next best thing. This chapter brought about a lot of personal conviction. Having four children with different personalities and different love languages can bring about some challenges in showing love individually. With children, it may sometimes be difficult to tell what their love language is; they all like gifts, they usually love to be praised, and they probably enjoy when you do something meaningful for them. But if you become intentional and really try to discover what their dominant love language is, you will notice the things that really make them feel loved.

My daughter Sade's dominant love language is quality time, and this usually involves a large amount of talking. I remember one day she said to me "Mommy, I want to tell you something." I said, "Of course, what's up?" She responded by saying, "I want to tell you something, but I don't have anything to say." What I wanted to really say was, "Well keep quiet then." It's obvious right? If you have nothing to say, then just don't say anything. But that would have absolutely crushed her. Love takes sacrifice… so I ignored all the emotions and exhaustion I was experiencing and said, "Well if you think long enough, I'm sure you will remember something exciting you want to tell me." I had to read between the lines and realize she was saying, "Mommy I really want to spend time with you right now, I wish I could think of something exciting to share with you, but I can't...so I'll just tell you so you can know how I feel."

With a large family, cooking is a time that I usually would prefer to have to myself and just unwind. But every time I am cooking and Sade is around, she wants to help. There she goes seeking that quality time again. Many times when I want to get dinner on the table quickly, I would have just told her no she can't help right now. I knew she was probably going to slow me down and make a bigger mess than I would make on my own; and the goal was to finish quickly, right? We need to eat so that we can get into bed; after all, school is in the morning. Doesn't saying no make sense? If there is one thing, I've learned from this most recent pandemic, is that life and routine can switch up instantly. And then, what's next? When everything pretty much worldwide had shut down, there was nothing to really rush for or no place to rush to. That's when many people rediscovered family; family meals, family drives, family games...etc. We were pretty much forced to, as we weren't allowed to go anywhere. But whatever the reason, kids and parents were reuniting and spending time together. It was during this time I also began to set aside time for us to "do things together"- specifically cooking and baking. I realized that there is probably going to be a mess afterwards and it is more than likely going to take longer than if I tackled it myself. But I also realized that "making dinner with mom" is more appreciated than "having mom make dinner for me".

Now, that life is returning to normal, there isn't as much

disposable time to do activities every day. But realizing that this is how my daughter feels loved, it pushes me to make the effort and plan baking activities ahead of time. I want my children to grow up knowing without a doubt that they are loved, and to provide them with a great example of what love is and looks like.

Showing love isn't always easy when your babies are no longer as "cute". When their personalities begin to develop and there are certain actions that they perform that warrant a raised eyebrow and a head turn. They may no longer seem as "cute" and though you know for certain that you love them, showing them this love during these situations may sometimes become more difficult. Here is where we need to be more intentional about it.

One very vivid memory I have is when Jayden and Sade asked why I loved Haylie and Josiah more than them. I told them that wasn't true and asked why they thought that I did. Their response was because "Haylie and Josiah don't have to clean up their messes" and they "don't get punished". I explained to Jayden and Sade that it's because I do love them that they have more responsibilities as they get older and consequences when they break rules. They probably only understood a little bit of what I said, but with time I am sure that they will get it. This is the part of showing love that is not always fun for parent or child - but necessary. Many rules that we make now for our children, may not be understood until much later, but we know that we have their best interest at heart.

Jayden loves to be affirmed. He loves to know that he is pleasing his family. Many times, when he is being disciplined, I must step back and think about how what I'm about to say would make him feel as I don't want to crush his spirits. A successful discipline session with him usually takes a bit of extra time and a bit of the "sandwich method". He needs to be assured that everything that he is doing isn't wrong; that he just made a mistake and that it is ok once he does his best to correct it. Even God himself chastises us but does so out of love.

The Bible says that God is a loving father, but He is also a consuming fire. He is a God that comforts, but also a God that chastises. But what if He only showed us his rough side? What if we were never exposed to the soft side of God's love, and only got to experience the wrath? We probably wouldn't believe that God loves us.

Psalm 86: 15 shows the compassionate side of our Father:

"But You, O Lord, are a God full of compassion, and gracious, long-suffering and abundant in mercy and truth."

Hebrew 12:6 displays our God as a God of order:

"- the Lord disciplines the one he loves and chastises every son whom he receives."

Just as God both shows mercy and yet chastises when necessary, is how we must raise our children to be emotionally sound yet disciplined adults. May God grant us grace to discern which gesture of love we should be showing to our children during various situations.

8

Sit Down and Be Still

This Chapter is about communing with God. Being silent and in tune with God to ensure that your steps are being ordered by Him.

If you have a child or children four years or older, more than likely you have said to them to "sit down and be still" a few or more times before. Perhaps they were too loud for the environment that you were in, or perhaps they were just a bit too wound up and needed to settle for a while. Sometimes children can get so excited running around that they commit certain actions without thinking about the consequences that resultantly ends in a chaos and messes that might have been avoided. Maybe you just wanted your children to be still for a bit so that you could have a moment to think without getting distracted. God is saying the same thing to us. "Be still my child".

Many times, we get so caught up being the busy mom, that we lose sight of the things we should normally be able to key in on; or maybe we focus on the wrong things. Running here, running there; driving the children from one activity to the next; cooking, cleaning, running errands and on and on. Of course, these are things that must get done. But many mothers are practically running on fumes trying to keep up with the demands of life. Struggling to find the balance between wife, mom, friend, sister, daughter, committee member, soccer mom, etc. Often, we find ourselves doing things that we "think" we should do; that we "think" would help, but God didn't ask us to do these things. We can sometimes place extra stress and pressure on ourselves, trying to do so many things that are not a part of "God's perfect will for our lives". We unknowingly go around creating the same avoidable chaos and mess that we scold our children for making. Well, not exactly the same type of mess, but it can be avoided if we were able to "sit down and be still" for a bit and tune in to Our Father.

Running around performing extra tasks that are not a part of God's plan for your life, that don't fit in the "job description" you have been given places extra stress and demands on you that may be above the grace of God on your life. When we do this, the tasks that we are required to perform become even more stressful because we are so overwhelmed with randomness.

I'm by no means downplaying the challenges that come along with motherhood but rather, trying to paint a picture of how stressful motherhood can be if and when we are not tuned in to God, and without involving Him in the planning process. For instance, God said He would not put more on us than we can bear; if we believe His word, then we ought to be able to fulfill all that He has called us to do. If we are unable to fulfil these tasks, then we are more than likely working above the level of grace that God has given us. Perhaps we have voluntarily added some responsibilities to our to-do lists that He did not ask us to. It's time to stop running. Sit still for a bit. It's time to tune in and recharge. It's time to compare God's list with our list. It's time for quiet.

Ok, you are probably thinking how in the world will I find quiet? How can you tell a mother to sit in silence? Did you forget that mothers have children? Where am I going to find quiet in my home?

These questions are awfully familiar to me. For a long time, I made excuses that if only my house wasn't so loud, I would be much further ahead. It would be much easier to find time for God. I would be able to wake up and spend hours with God, receiving revelation after revelation. I thought oh well, once the kids get older, I can revisit this; after all these are God's children, right? He knows that He made them very loud. If He wants me to find time to spend with Him, He will create the time for me. It was a lie! A BIG one.

I had to first understand, that me not spending quiet time to think and to listen for God's instruction is what was creating more chaos in my life. Making excuses and blaming the children for "being loud" will not solve the problem. I had to get creative and find the time. If nothing else, my sanity was dependent on it. I had to push away the feelings of guilt that tried to surge because I was creating time for myself when so many other people needed me. I'm sure you have heard all the sayings before; "You can't pour from an empty cup"; "You can't give what you don't have". "You can't charge someone else's battery if yours is dead". I had heard them all as well, but the understanding wasn't there. Or maybe I refused to acknowledge it. I thank God for spiritual authority and Godly connections who have helped me to understand the importance of having regular quiet time and staying constantly connected to Him. It was time to get creative. Now that I understood what was needed, how was I going to find the time to make it happen. The time was right there in front of me all along, I just needed to adjust a few things, switch my schedule around a bit, and things began to fall into place.

For instance, by God's grace we own a day spa. It's peaceful and quiet there. It must be as people are coming there to relax and get away from the busyness of life. I figure that if our clients can escape to the peaceful oasis that we very strategically created, then so can I! The spa was intentionally created as a peaceful space for people to forget about what is going on in the world, in their life, even if just for a short time. I also needed to do this; why not take advantage of the environment for myself. Instead of just going to the spa for the purpose of work (when there were appointments scheduled for me, or to oversee the staff) I created set days where no matter what happened, once I take the kids to school, I will go straight to the spa. I would not begin work right away, but I would spend time with God. You would be surprised at the amount of revelation a person can receive by just being silent and tuned in to God. Life is busy. The world can be loud. There is so much information that we take in daily voluntarily as well as involuntarily. All this information can cloud our judgement, can cause God's voice to be muffled. If we don't spend quiet time with God regularly, when He is attempting to get our attention during "the noise", it will be very difficult to recognize that it is Him.

There is an example that I heard a while back, that I believe will help. Imagine you are at a very loud sporting event, and your spouse starts calling your name. You may not recognize that someone is calling you at first, but when you hear your name, you will more than likely recognize your spouse's voice. Because you two have spent time together and you have gotten to know your spouse well, recognizing their voice amongst the other voices would be easy. This is the same with God. There is no way that we will be confident in what He is saying to us if we cannot first recognize His voice. We need to be able to hear and know God's sound when He calls, when He speaks.

God did not intend for mothering to be hard. He never intended for us to struggle alone. He wants to help us, and He has been trying to get our attention for a long time. Finding time to be still and listen will be imperative in successful child rearing. In fact, the time was there all along. God gave us time. We must ask the Holy Spirit to teach us to manage our time skillfully. Do not feel guilty for putting others aside for God; even if it is your husband or your own children that God has blessed you with.

As mothers, we many times overlook our needs and desires to fulfil the needs and desires of others, starting with our immediate family. While motherhood calls for great sacrifice, we are first called to "Love one another, AS we love ourselves" (Matthew 22:39). It is not a crime nor is it a sin to have time to yourself to commune with God. It is not a crime to forget everyone else's wants for a short time to ensure that you are tuned in with the Father. Not only will you be recharged and more energized, but as the Holy Spirit whispers secrets and directions for your family and children, you will be silent and attentive enough to hear and receive. Even when you return to your daily routine, His voice would be more familiar to you and you will hear Him give directions, though it's not completely silent.

Think about it, if God created us, and created our kids (and He did), why wouldn't we go to Him and ask Him what to do and how to do it? If we truly understood that these are God's children, His gifts, and we are meant to be stewards of them for a short time, it really would take the pressure and a lot of self-placed responsibility off of us as mothers. If you were babysitting someone's child or children for the first time, wouldn't you ask the parents about their family procedures, rules, and expectations for you as their temporary guardian? Wouldn't it be important to know how they would approach certain situations?

Think about yourself as a guardian of your children; a long-term guardian that is. As much excitement and connection that you may have experienced when planning for and giving birth to your little ones, they really don't belong to you. Especially if you have had them blessed and presented back to God...you are merely stewards over them. Having this small bit of detachment from our kids can provide us the freedom needed that would allow us to "train them up" (Prov. 22:6) into exactly who God wants them to be.

So how do we know what to do? How do we know which direction to lead our children? How can we as moms prevent running around, running "crazy" trying to keep up with life? *Sit down and be quiet.* The same thing that we constantly tell our kids to do all day. Slow down for a bit and listen to what God is saying to you daily. He is not only a long-term master planner, but also a short term one as well. Psalm 119:105 says: "Thy word is a lamp to your feet, and a light unto my path. Psalm 119:105" God is there to direct us every step of the way. Stop running around long enough to ask Him what you should do and then actually LISTEN to what He says. That is, apply The Word. Be a doer. (James 1:22)

The Bible tells us in James 4:2 that "...we have not because we ask not". Is it really that simple? Absolutely! God is not the author of confusion; if you take the time to ask Him how He would have you raise His children, He will definitely answer! Be it directly, through a message, or by nudging you to get advice from a mentor; He will answer. The challenge for us moms, is being silent enough to wait for an answer. Sometimes God wants to give us the answer right there but, in our busyness, we end our commune before He can respond. Other times He sends the answer later, but we miss it because we are just "caught up". Maybe we haven't spent enough time getting familiar with God's voice, so when He tries to get out attention through the crowd, we don't recognize His voice. The sound is not familiar to us.

Let's push pass having to look back in hindsight saying, "I had a feeling about that!" As not every time He gives us the opportunity for a do-over. Let's normalize being "still" periodically and hearing God's voice whenever He speaks.

9

Hide and Seek

One, two, three, four, five, six, seven, eight, nine, ten...ready or not, here I come! This chapter is about overall parenting and the challenges that come with it.

Whether you are ready or not...there will be trials! So, let's get ready, the challenges are coming!

Wait, can we ever really be ready? How can we get ready to go somewhere, and we don't really know where "somewhere" is? Well, that's what parenting is, right? A journey with lots of unexpected twists and turns in hopes to end up at a destination with respectable, successful, praiseworthy children that have indeed made you proud, and our Father up above ecstatic! Three words for you... "The Holy Spirit". It is literally ONLY the Holy Spirit that keeps me going many days when these "ready or not, here I come" moments occur. I honestly do not know how people "mother" without Jesus these days! It's only by the grace of God that I have been able to control my emotions when being pushed by one of my beloved children. Sometimes it feels like they conspire together and say, "Let's all push mommy's buttons; let's see how she reacts today!" In all sincerity, many times, I don't get it right, but the times that I do, it is not by my strength, but by the grace of God.

There are so many different types and levels to challenges that will occur throughout the rearing of our children. I have talked to many mothers with children in different age groups and they all have shared different situations that they were experiencing or have experienced with their children. I remember my response to a mother with teenagers being, "wait, it doesn't stop?!". No, it doesn't! Just, like the challenges we face in life, as soon as we win one, another pops up. But we continue fighting. Well, that's what champions do, fight and win! And there are no exceptions for us supermoms! We win gracefully because we have the Holy Spirit guiding us every step of the way.

> *Romans 8:14 (New Living Translation) states, "For all who are led by the Spirit of God are children of God."*

As Christian supermoms we have a special superpower that when we take the time to use it, our parenting experience would be much smoother and more enjoyable. God has given us the opportunity to ask Him anything! To ask what to do in every unexpected situation. We can go to God and ask, "what do you want my child to become?"; "What school should we send them to?". "Should we enroll our children in karate?" etc. But what about when your child unexpectedly screams at you or you get an unexpected call from a teacher saying that your child was in a fight? What do you do then? You didn't raise them like this! Now, by God's grace these things will never happen with your child or children; but we must remember that their destiny is so great that the enemy is going to try everything possible to knock them off course and get you to say the wrong thing to them - to speak damnation over them. It's very easy to let our emotions get the best of us, but if we choose to listen to the Holy Spirit over our feelings, we will truly come out successful.

I'll give you an example. My children attend a Christian based school, and I was helping my eldest son with his scripture reflection questions. I would ask him what he thinks the answer is, expecting a response and prepared to elaborate to help him understand. He kept saying "I don't know! I don't know!" I was getting extremely annoyed and almost angry. He is very bright, and I knew he understood the scripture and knew how to answer the questions. The Holy Spirit said to me, "Just give him a minute. He is just upset because you made him turn the TV off. He will get over it soon." Oh, but did I listen? Nah... I was deep in my feelings and decided to keep pushing and pushing, till I realized I was completely raising my voice, telling him "You know the answer to this! Why are you telling me you don't?" Over and repeatedly; we were getting nowhere! The Holy Spirit knew that this would not be successful, hence He told me to wait a while. But how dare I accept "I don't know" for an answer from my child? Well, this went on until I obliged to the instruction. But by this time, we were both upset that continuing on with the assignment was pointless, so I called it a night. I totally ignored the insight from the Holy Spirit and had messed up.

The Holy Spirit had literally told me what to do to ensure a positive outcome and I believed that my way was better. I then repented acknowledging my wrong and my unnecessary need to use my authority wrongfully at that time. Of course, we can't go back in time, but I repented and moved on; vowing to obey that still small voice the next time.

It's this same Holy Spirit, that you can go to and ask, "How should I handle this? My son never gets into fights! Lord what is this about? I don't know what to do Father, please tell me what to do!". And if we learn to control our emotions and wait, it's the same Holy Spirit who would give us the secrets on what to do.

> *Matthew 10:3 says, "But even the hairs of your head are all numbered." If the Father knows exactly how many hairs are on our heads, don't you think He knows how to handle a little situation?*

Parenting challenges are not new. And they are not going anywhere; they will just be constantly changing. But God never changes! He sent His Holy Spirit to guide us and to help us succeed in every situation. The Bible says that God is the same yesterday, today, and forever. He knew how to handle the situations that have happened before, the present ones, and the ones that will surely come. Don't mother alone, The Holy Spirit is there to be our guide... let Him guide!

10

No More Training Wheels

This chapter is about balance. Using the Holy Spirit to ensure that you remain upright and steady.

Ok, so quick disclosure, I still cannot ride a bike. I'm sure if I really wanted to learn and I tried now, that God will give me the grace and I could become the best bike rider ever – but I figure I can drive a car, so no need to ride a bike.

Anyway, so back to balance. The Oxford dictionary defines balance as "an even distribution of weight enabling someone or something to remain upright and steady." As mothers, there is indeed a lot of weight that we are responsible for distributing while we are expected to remain steady. Let's begin with a practical example – balancing the needs of all the members of your family.

STILL STANDING - 49

Come and join me at an evening at home after a long day of work, school, and day care. Everyone barely gets in the door, and then it starts.

Josiah: "Mommy! Snack! Snack!" (because he believes eating should always be first on his list.)

Haylie: Crying... (Because she absolutely loves to be cuddled ALL the time and has probably been spoiled at daycare, but nobody can cuddle with her right now)

Sadé: "You wouldn't BELIEVE what happened at school today!" (Because she is dramatic and loves to talk and whatever happened is a pretty big deal to her.)

Jayden: "Josiah! No! Can someone come for Josiah please! He is messing up my stuff!" (Because I haven't had a chance yet to get Josiah's "snack", so he found his way into some of Jayden's gadgets.)

Alex: "Babe, you wouldn't believe who called me today! I give you 3 tries" (Because Sadé gets all her drama from him and he clearly also thinks this is important to talk about right now.)

Me: Josiah leave Jayden's things alone please, come for your snack; Haylie I'm coming baby! Sadé and Jayden come and move your bags from in front of the door please!

Sadé: So, are you going to guess?

Alex: I guess you didn't hear me...

Me: (in my head... "we're having pizza tonight bruh")

And...this...is...just...one.... aspect! So, what do you do? As a mother, how do you handle everyone's individual needs? Overtime I've learned that for one, I don't have to do everything myself. While there are some needs that may only be able to be met by me, I've learnt to delegate and ask for help. Just because it may be our job to ensure that everything keeps running smoothly in a family, doesn't mean that the mother must do everything herself.

Now, let me first say, there is no cookie cutter manual on how to run your household. Every family has different dynamics; that would mean that they must handle situations differently from another family. Let me also say, by no means, am I a Pinterest mom (no disrespect). I do not have all the meal preparation and arts and craft sessions figured out. But being completely dependent on the Holy Spirit has provided tips and insight on how we should run our family.

So, back to the terribly busy evening. How did I handle that? Well, I originally wanted to prepare a home cooked meal for my family, but I had to fill in at work, when I thought I would have been at home and able to prep. Before time, I would have beat myself up about spending extra money, eating processed food and so on and so forth. But being sensitive to the present dynamics going on that evening, I picked my battle and opted to order the pizza.

Me: "Babe, I heard you. Give me a sec please. Oh, can you see what Haylie wants? I'm going in here to Sadé, and we're having pizza tonight."
Everyone: "Yay Pizza!"
My reaction: Rolls eyes, as if my home cooked meals aren't tasty... anyway now everyone is on their best behavior because they love pizza nights – especially the spontaneous ones and I

don't have to cook; a win-win. (And I don't feel guilty about it either.)

So, what's my point? Basically, sometimes we must learn to roll with the punches. Adjust plans when necessary. A big part about balance is what is important at the present time; what carries the most weight? Who or what needs the most attention now or first? What can be eliminated right now to ensure that you as mom remain "upright and steady"? Not uptight and unstable. Of course, a nutritious home cooked meal is always going to be healthier, but since I chose to go to work (adding something to my plate that was not there prior), and lost my prep time, I must now balance the scale by taking something else off to ensure that I remain "upright and steady".

Also, take note, that though you are only one person, and cannot meet everyone's need at the same time, it's important to acknowledge the need and attend to it once you are freed up. By God's grace, I did get to hear Sadé's story, and totally guessed on the first try who it was that called Alex (I always guess right, and he still gets shocked that I do.)

The scripture recorded in Ecclesiastes 3: 1-8, gives us an explicit view of time and balance. Read below as recorded by the New Living Translation version.

For everything there is a season, a time for every activity under heaven. A time to be born and a time to die. A time to plant and a time to harvest. A time to kill and a time to heal. A time to tear down and a time to build up. A time to cry and a time to laugh. A time to grieve and a time to dance. A time to scatter stones and a time to gather stones. A time to embrace and a time to turn away. A time to search and a time to quit searching. A time to keep and a time to throw away. A time to tear and a time to mend. A time to be quiet and a time to speak. A time to love and a time to hate. A time for war and a time for peace.

2019 was truly a year where I learned first-hand about balance. I was an esthetic instructor, a massage therapy student. a wife, a leader in church, oh and a mom. As a matter of fact, when I started school, Josiah was 2 months old. Oh, talk about demands from all around! This is one time that I really had to decipher what was the most pressing at any given time. Sometimes, it was homework, other times, it was planning for my students, lots of times it involved nursing a newborn; but sometimes it was just watching a movie with the family. I cannot take any credit for coming out of that season successful. It was only by the grace of God. The Holy Spirit was indeed my helper! He knew that I had a lot going on and He helped me navigate the distribution of weight in order to remain "upright and steady".

I wish I can provide advice about meal prepping, creating schedules, and prioritizing but I honestly can't. Remaining balanced was all God's doing. Sometimes I felt as graceful as a ballerina on her toes, and other times (many other times) I felt like a clumsy waitress attempting to catch a tray of glasses before it hit the ground. But He kept me.

Now, don't get me wrong, I did plan. I did create schedules. But it wasn't a cookie cutter experience. Even planning felt overwhelming at times; but The Holy Spirit indeed helped me. As much as I wanted to just mimic a video on meal prep or creating schedules; it only worked when I involved the Holy Spirit. He knew what type of planning I would stick to; what would work for my family. He knew.

He sent destiny helpers for my family, told me what to study for my exams, He sent favor with tuition; everything was divinely orchestrated. Talk to God. He knows everything you have going on. He knows what your family dynamic is like. He knows what is in every glass that you are trying to carry. He also knows how you should position every glass on that tray so you can carry it like a graceful ballerina.

11

I Can Do All Things

In this chapter I share about our limitations and God's unlimited ability.

Listen, parenting isn't the easiest thing to do. You are raising at least one other human being, with his/her own personality, to be successful in this ever-changing world; simultaneously, while maybe trying to keep up with your job, husband, and maintaining your mind. I get it. This is not an easy task. Please be nice to yourself, you hold many roles and titles. But you can do it. Keep pushing!

Let me emphasize that: you CAN do it. Now, I'm not referring to the random roles you decided to pick up because you didn't know how to say NO, or you thought would make you more accepted in the "mommy" groups. I'm referring to the specific visions God has given you to fulfill. While there may be some moms specifically called to stay at home and raise their kids, (and that is their God given purpose during the child rearing years) there are others who have opted to take this route just because "life is too hard" or maybe they genuinely just don't know how to make "mothering" and pursuing dream work together. Deep down, I wanted to pursue more. I knew that I should be doing more, but just couldn't figure out how. I was relying on my own strength. Maybe this is your experience. Perhaps, you have suppressed your God given vision by picking up other "mommy activities" that haven't been directed by God. But you go ahead and do it any way to fill the void; to feel accomplished. This was totally me!

Prior to having kids, I was all about my career and pursuing my vision. I totally love the spa industry and was always thinking of new ideas to try out next or I was exploring how to remain at the top in the industry. When I was back home in The Bahamas and when I resided in Florida, I was present at every beauty and spa show and conference in South and Central Florida. I wanted to remain current with the latest in the industry! After I had Jayden, I didn't attend as many conferences as I used to but always tried to plan our family vacations around the dates for the conferences to ensure I wasn't getting totally left behind. When Sadé came, I continued in this direction; choosing one or two of the many spa events scheduled and combining it with vacation time.

However, by the time baby three had come, life presented a totally different dynamic. By then my family had relocated to Canada and the birth of Haylie had presented a whole new set of challenges. With my focus set on the challenges, I convinced myself that I'm probably going to be a stay-at-home mom "forever". Don't get me wrong, I still had my dreams...but I don't think I completely believed in myself or that God would allow them to come to fruition at this time, or anytime soon. So, I remained at home, and I complained a lot. I defied Apostle Paul's advice to the church at Philippi when he wrote "Do everything without complaining and arguing" (Philippians 2:14 NLT). I knew I would function better if I had childcare and went out to work, but I had already made up in my mind based on what I perceived to be unsurmountable challenges, no one can help the way I can (big lie). What deception! For a moment I held my pity party, drowning in my complaints, telling myself what is impossible, listening and partnering with the enemy's lies until...

It took constant reminders from my spiritual father about the promise God had given me for my life. To fulfil that promise, there was no way I could remain at home. I began to look for work, even though I knew most of the pay would be going to childcare; but I had to awake the giant in me that had fallen asleep for years.

I took on a position as an esthetics instructor for an Edmonton beauty school. Seeing the students learn new techniques and hearing their stories, I began to come alive. My interest and passion had been buried; constantly being smothered with the mismanaged overwhelming duties that came with being a mother of four. I didn't realize that I was letting my passions die. It took my husband's constant encouraging me to go to a spa conference in Las Vegas in 2019, where my passion was rekindled. I almost forewent the trip.

My sister and I had planned the trip together, and everything was set to go. Tickets were bought. Hotel was paid for; rental car booked. I was excited to see what was new in the industry.

The day before I was supposed to travel, the daycare called and said that Haylie was having a seizure and that my husband and I should take her straight to the emergency room at the hospital. Haylie had never had a seizure before but nonetheless she was admitted to the hospital. I knew deep down she was fine, and that God had her in the palm of His hands. There was really nothing that I could do, but I felt I would be judged as a "bad mother" if I still traveled knowing that she was hospitalized. That was literally the only reason that I was going to stay; to please the people that I thought would somehow find out my actions and "judge" me.

I was encouraged by my husband and my spiritual father to still travel as planned, and I am incredibly happy that I did. I later realized that this was a mere distraction from the enemy attempting to bury my dreams again. The hospital ran many tests and realized that Haylie hadn't had a seizure; the tests showed no signs of seizure activity. I would have once again missed an amazing opportunity for God to expand my career and make us business owners.

By God's grace, I can say today that He has given me the ability to wear many hats, and the grace to wear them well. I am not perfect, but I am humbled to know that He finds me capable to perform so many roles. I am grateful to God to be a wife and a mother of four. My career life includes owning and managing a day spa and providing esthetic and spa training. I am extremely humbled to also be able to serve as a leader in our church and author books as directed by the Holy Spirit. Is it easy all the time? Absolutely not! But rest assured, if God has called you to wear multiple hats, He has given you the grace to wear them well. I realize that when I feel stressed and overwhelmed, it's because I have probably added something to the list that He did not ask me to do. Either that or I am not tapping into the grace that He has given for these tasks. Being a mother is NOT an excuse to let your dreams and passions die.

You can be a great mother and still fulfill your God-given destiny. Now this looks different for everyone. Your destiny may not involve many roles. You may have been given one role. You may have also been called to be in the home and to homeschool your children. But whatever God has called you to do, know that you can do it, and you can do it well. Whatever He is requiring of you, God has placed everything you need inside of you to fulfil your dream. You have the access to achieve it. I challenge you to not only teach your children Philippians 4:13, "I can do all things through Christ who strengthens me" but demonstrate this passage for your children. Show your children that they can fulfil their God-given destiny. Teach your children that they must not allow anything to cause their dreams to die. Share your stories, your experiences – successes and failures – with your children. Let them know that

"God has good plans for their future and a hope" (Jeremiah 29:11)

and watch your children soar.

12

When Mommy?...Soon

This is probably one of the most sensitive topics in this book. This chapter is about Waiting…. specifically, waiting for a promise God has given about your child. Waiting for your child to clue in and "get it". Waiting for any positive sign that you are doing the right thing and moving in the right direction… that you are a good parent.

I've mentioned this earlier… I by no means felt capable of writing this book. Even though the information is inspired by the Holy Spirit, I'd still have to put my name on it right? Before and during this writing process I battled with negative thoughts of unworthiness of "helping others" while I felt like a failure. However, by God's grace I had to hold on to the fact, that though things may not physically look like it's all coming together yet, I was doing the best and my children would be successful and eventually they would appreciate my efforts. In the same way, we must do whatever it takes to hold onto every promise, God has sent to you about your child – whether written or prophetic. If you feel that He hasn't specifically sent a direct prophecy yet, you can always go to the word of God to find truth to keep moving forward. Search God's word for a scripture that is relevant to your situation, that depicts what you want your child's future to look like and stand on it. The Bible says in

> *Psalm 127:3 that "children are the heritage of the Lord" and in Proverbs 10:22 that "God gives blessings and adds no sorrow to it."*

I'll share a personal example. When Haylie was born, she suffered a brain injury due to an extended time without oxygen before she was delivered. God sent a prophecy "that just as He said let there be light and there was light, He said Haylie is healed and she was healed." He also gave me a scripture to hold on to, Corinthians 2: 5. I did not know what it said prior to that moment, but once I read it, I knew that it was for me.

> *" I did this so you would trust not in human wisdom but in the power of God."*

This scripture is what has kept me "still standing" after so many negative medical prognoses. God is faithful. He knew it would get intense and that I would need something to keep me going strong and holding faith.

That was about three years and ten months ago to date of me writing this section. (Oh, as I wrote this, I received a message from her developmental assistant that she was extremely happy today and had a good day! We celebrate all wins - big or small). There are presently about ten medical personnel involved in Haylie's care; numerous doctor's appointments; she has had four procedures requiring her to go under general anesthesia; she still requires complete assistance for all her care and is mostly tube fed. But who am I to challenge God's word? He said what He said... and "His promises are yes and Amen" (2 Corinthians 1:20). So, what do I do? I believe. Carry on with life and wait. Sounds easy right? Nope. It's not. Sometimes the physical demands are a lot to bear. Sometimes, the emotions try to get in the way of living freely. Many times, it's the mental aspect. I'm naturally a very logical person. Faith and logic don't tend to go well hand in hand. Fighting the negative thoughts that remind me of the facts over and over can be exhausting at times. But knowing that God's truth prevails above the facts, is always comforting.

Then there is the aspect of time. God has His own time. He is completely in control. He said He healed her, and He said she would recover...but He didn't say when. Based on her purpose however, things must change for her to fulfill it. So, we play our part and then we wait. This aspect of parenting is extremely hard, especially for mothers. Knowing what we want to see our children doing, knowing what they ought to be doing, but it just hasn't happened yet. How do we hold on?

Do we hold on? Does it make sense to even believe anymore? What if it doesn't happen?

Ok, let's put it like this. What if you choose not to believe? Then more than likely, the promise will not be fulfilled. But why not choose to believe? Why not give God a chance to blow your mind? There is literally no situation too big for God to change! Whether it has to do with healing, bringing a wayward child back, or just literally waiting for a specific prophesy spoken over their life to come to fruition; If God said it, it MUST happen. The Bible said in

Isaiah 55:11 that "God's word will not return to Him void."

I've made up my mind that I'm going to believe that change is coming until I physically see the change manifested. I've made up my mind as hard as it is to keep believing, I will keep believing. I've made up my mind that when I don't want to believe, I will keep believing. I have nothing to lose holding on to God's word, but if I give up now, I lose everything! Every chance of a miracle; every chance of seeing the manifestation; every chance of being a vessel for others to see God's glory and being drawn closer to Him.

I encourage you to hold on. Hang in there. If you feel like you are hanging on by a thin thread, keep hanging! When you feel like trusting God doesn't make sense anymore, that's when you need to trust Him the most. Everything you need is in Him. He is the only one that can turn around what is deemed impossible!

   Healing is coming!
   Your child will be great!
   Your children will fulfill every God given purpose!
   That child will return home!

If you are reading this and your thoughts are:

"You don't know my situation..."
"This one is really bad..."
"They said that it's permanent..."

I'll remind you firstly that God is the same yesterday, today and forever; this means the miracles He performed back then, He can perform now. Secondly, let's look a little bit at the resume of our never changing God. You have more than likely heard all these before, but reminders are always good.

Lazarus was dead for four days. His heart had stopped. His brain had stopped. His body was decomposing. It stank! Yet Jesus simply told Him to walk to come to Him, and He came! The woman with the issue of blood had been bleeding nonstop for twelve years! She was probably extremely weak, and more than likely smelling foul as well. She had faith that even though she had tried everything and everyone and nothing has helped, if she could just drag herself a little further and merely touch the hem of Jesus' garment, that she would be made well!

There are stories after stories after stories of miracles in the bible that we can use for examples. But I will just use one more story to tie it all together.

David was the youngest of eight sons. But he was confident in the power of God. He explains in 1 Samuel 17:34-36 that whenever a lion or bear comes and take a sheep from his flock, he would go after it and snatch it back, and kill it if it tried to attack him. We are talking about lions and bears - extremely strong animals. But it's David's confidence in God I want to concentrate on. Because he knew God's performance history (that whatever He said He will do He will do), facing Goliath was not an issue for him; in fact, it seemed small. He was facing a huge, seemingly impossible situation, but he was faithful that if God's power worked before, it will work again; and it did!

I challenge you to tap into the miracles that God has already performed for you and your family. Look up testimonies about your current situation and whether you are holding on by a thick rope, or thin thread... continue to hold on.

Psalm 30:5 "...Weeping may endure for a night, but joy comes in the morning"

Meet Shuranda

Born in Nassau, Bahamas, Shuranda lives in Edmonton in Alberta, Canada with her husband Alexander, and four children Jayden, Sadé, Haylie, and Josiah. She is a Medical Esthetician and Registered Massage Therapist by trade and has a great passion for the beauty, spa, and wellness industry. She is the co-owner of Retreat 2 Paradise Wellness Spa Corp. and Damara Day Spa Edmonton where she loves to pamper, encourage, and educate. Shuranda is a leader at Cornerstone Christian of God Edmonton, where she credits much of her spiritual growth.

www.ingramcontent.com/pod-product-compliance
Lightning Source LLC
Chambersburg PA
CBHW062152100526
44589CB00014B/1803